BONAIRE
TRAVEL GUIDE

Your Guide to Diving, Beaches, and Island Serenity: Discover Adventure in the Caribbean Netherlands (Full-color)

MILES LARKWOOD

Disclaimer

The information in this travel guide to Bonaire has been thoroughly researched and is accurate at the time of publication. However, travel conditions, local businesses, and attractions can change without notice. The author and publisher make no guarantees regarding the accuracy, completeness, or current relevance of the content.

Readers are advised to verify important details independently, including travel restrictions, operating hours, and safety guidelines. The author and publisher shall not be held liable for any loss, inconvenience, or damage resulting from the use of this guide.

Travel responsibly and enjoy your journey!

Gratitude

Writing this guide to Bonaire has been an extraordinary journey, and it wouldn't have been possible without the support, insights, and warm hospitality of so many incredible people.

First and foremost, my heartfelt thanks go to the locals of Bonaire, whose kindness and generosity brought this island's vibrant spirit to life. A special mention goes to Maria and Carlos at the Rincon Market for sharing their stories and pointing me to the island's best-kept secrets—from the freshest local cuisine to the hidden snorkeling spots.

To Anna, my adventurous travel companion, thank you for your boundless enthusiasm as we kayaked through mangroves, explored the salt flats, and soaked in Bonaire's mesmerizing sunsets. Your keen sense of wonder made every experience unforgettable.

A sincere thanks to the team at the Bonaire Tourism Office for their invaluable tips and unwavering patience in answering my many questions. Your passion for preserving the island's culture and natural beauty inspired every page of this guide.

Finally, to you, my reader: this book is your key to discovering Bonaire's magic. Thank you for letting me be part of your journey. I hope you experience the same awe, joy, and connection that this special island gave to me.

Here's to adventure, exploration, and unforgettable memories.

<u>About the Author</u>

Miles Larkwood is a passionate travel writer dedicated to uncovering the world's most captivating destinations and sharing them with intrepid explorers. With a wealth of experience roaming Europe's picturesque towns, breathtaking coastlines, and vibrant cultural hubs, Miles blends practical tips with engaging storytelling to create guides that both inspire and inform.

Fascinated by local traditions, history, and the art of slow travel, Miles strives to make every journey meaningful and accessible for readers. Whether hiking Madeira's scenic levadas, exploring hidden corners of a bustling city, or savoring a glass of regional wine, Miles immerses himself fully in the essence of each destination.

Through thoughtfully crafted travel guides, Miles Larkwood invites you to discover the beauty of the world, one adventure at a time, bringing the spirit of exploration to life with every page.

Contents

1. Welcome to Bonaire

An overview of Bonaire

Let's start by introducing Bonaire, a Caribbean island unlike any other. Located just off the coast of Venezuela, Bonaire is part of the Caribbean Netherlands. It's known for its calm vibe, beautiful nature, and a deep respect for the environment.

A Bit of History

Bonaire has a fascinating past. The island was originally home to the Caquetío people, part of the Arawak tribe, who arrived here over a thousand years ago. They lived peacefully, fishing and farming, until the Spanish claimed the island in the 1500s. After a few changes in power, Bonaire became part of the Dutch Kingdom in the 17th century, where it remains today.

Salt production played a big role in the island's history. If you visit, you'll see large white salt pyramids and pink-colored salt flats—a reminder of the hard work done by enslaved people centuries ago.

A Blend of Cultures

What makes Bonaire so special is the mix of cultures you'll find here. The island has Dutch roots, but it's also deeply Caribbean, with influences from Africa, South America, and the neighboring islands. The locals speak Papiamentu, a Creole language that reflects this blend, along with Dutch and English.

You'll notice this cultural mix in the food, music, and celebrations. From traditional dances to lively festivals, Bonaire's culture is full of energy and pride.

The Geography

Bonaire is a small island, about 24 miles long and 5 miles wide. It's surrounded by clear turquoise water and colorful coral reefs that make it a favorite spot for divers and snorkelers. On land, you'll find rugged hills, cactus-filled landscapes, and peaceful beaches. The island is also home to some unique wildlife, like flamingos and iguanas.

There's something calming about Bonaire's natural beauty. It's the kind of place where you can truly relax, but there's also plenty to explore. From underwater adventures to hiking trails, there's no shortage of experiences waiting for you.

So, welcome to Bonaire—an island with a rich past, vibrant culture, and breathtaking scenery. You're in for an unforgettable experience.

Why Bonaire is a Unique Destination in the Caribbean

Bonaire isn't like other Caribbean islands that are packed with big resorts and endless crowds. It has a more laid-back and intimate feel, which is one of the main reasons people fall in love with it. Here's what makes Bonaire stand out:

A Diver's Dream
Bonaire is famous around the world for its diving and snorkeling. The entire coastline is a protected marine park, which means the coral reefs and marine life are in incredible shape. Whether you're an experienced diver or just learning, Bonaire offers easy access to some of the best underwater spots in the Caribbean. Many of these sites are right off the shore, so you don't even need a boat to start exploring.

A Focus on Nature
Unlike busier destinations, Bonaire is deeply committed to preserving its natural beauty. The island isn't overdeveloped, and you won't find towering hotels or sprawling shopping malls. Instead, you'll see salt flats, mangroves, and open spaces. Washington Slagbaai National Park takes up about 20% of the island and is a haven for wildlife like flamingos, parrots, and wild goats.

A Quiet Escape
Bonaire is the place to go if you're looking for peace and quiet. There are no cruise ship terminals or flashy nightlife districts. Instead, you'll find calm beaches, friendly locals, and a slower pace of life. It's the perfect destination for people who want to recharge and enjoy the simple pleasures of nature and community.

Outdoor Adventures
Even though it's small, Bonaire offers plenty of adventure. Windsurfing at Lac Bay is a must-try, thanks to the steady breezes and shallow waters. Kiteboarding is another popular activity, as are kayaking and paddleboarding in the mangroves. If you prefer to stay on land, there are hiking trails, mountain biking paths, and even caves to explore.

Rich Culture in a Small Package
Bonaire may be peaceful, but it's far from boring. Its unique mix of Dutch, African, and Caribbean influences gives the island a distinct personality. Local festivals, like Bonaire Day or the colorful Carnival, bring people together in celebration. Plus, the island's food scene is surprisingly diverse, with everything from fresh seafood to dishes inspired by Dutch and South American flavors.

In short, Bonaire offers a rare combination of natural beauty, adventure, and culture. It's a place where you can feel connected to the earth and sea while enjoying the warm, welcoming vibe of a tight-knit community. That's what makes it one-of-a-kind in the Caribbean.

When to Visit: Weather and Peak Seasons

Bonaire is a year-round destination, thanks to its warm and sunny climate. The island sits outside the hurricane belt, so you don't have to worry about tropical storms disrupting your plans. However, depending on what you're looking for in your trip, some times of the year might be better for you than others.

The Weather

Bonaire has a tropical climate, which means it's warm all year, with temperatures usually hovering between 77°F and 88°F (25°C to 31°C). The trade winds keep things comfortable, even on hotter days. Rainfall is minimal, and when it does rain, it's usually quick and happens in the early morning or late evening.

The "rainy season" runs from October to January, but don't let that scare you off. Showers are short, and the island stays green and beautiful. Plus, you might score lower accommodation prices during this time.

Peak Tourist Season: December to April

If you love a lively atmosphere and don't mind paying a bit more, this is the time to visit. The weather is perfect, and many travelers from colder climates flock to Bonaire for some sunshine. Popular diving spots, restaurants, and beaches might be a bit busier, so booking accommodations and tours in advance is a good idea.

Off-Peak Season: May to November

This is Bonaire's quieter period. It's warmer, but the trade winds make it pleasant. If you prefer fewer crowds, this is the ideal time to visit. Plus, prices for flights and accommodations tend to drop, so you can stretch your budget further. Diving visibility is excellent year-round, so you won't miss out on the island's main attraction.

Special Considerations

Diving Events: If you're into scuba diving, keep an eye on local events like Bonaire Dive Week, which usually takes place in September. It's a great way to meet other divers and enjoy special activities.

Flamingos and Wildlife: If you're a nature lover, visit between February and July when the flamingos are nesting at Pekelmeer Sanctuary.

No matter when you go, Bonaire's relaxed vibe and natural beauty ensure a memorable trip. The key is to choose the time that fits your travel style—whether you're seeking quiet solitude or a social scene.

Entry Requirements and Travel Tips

Before packing your bags for Bonaire, it's a good idea to make sure you're ready for a smooth trip. The entry requirements are straightforward, and with a few travel tips, you'll be well-prepared to enjoy your stay.

Entry Requirements

Passport: A valid passport is required for all visitors, and it should be valid for at least six months beyond your travel dates.

Visa: Visitors from most countries, including the U.S., Canada, and EU nations, don't need a visa for stays up to 90 days. If you're unsure about your country's requirements, check with the nearest Dutch embassy or consulate.

ED Card: Before you arrive, you'll need to complete Bonaire's Electronic Health Declaration (ED) Card online. This form is quick to fill out and helps speed up the arrival process.

Return Ticket: You may be asked to show proof of a return or onward ticket when entering the island.

Travel Insurance: While not mandatory, travel insurance that includes health coverage is strongly recommended.

Tourist Tax: Bonaire has a mandatory Visitor Entry Tax of $75 per person (as of 2024). This tax helps fund local infrastructure and environmental conservation. You can pay it online before your trip or upon arrival at the airport. Make sure to keep your receipt handy, as you may need to show proof of payment during your stay.

Health and Safety Tips

Vaccinations: No specific vaccinations are required for entry. However, it's always a good idea to ensure routine immunizations are up-to-date.

Sun Protection: The Caribbean sun is strong, so pack sunscreen, a hat, and sunglasses to protect yourself. Reef-safe sunscreen is essential to help preserve Bonaire's marine environment.

Stay Hydrated: The heat can sneak up on you, so drink plenty of water throughout the day.

Travel Tips

Currency: Bonaire uses the U.S. dollar (USD), so there's no need to exchange currency if you're coming from the U.S. Credit cards are widely accepted, but having some cash on hand for smaller purchases is always a good idea.

Language: The locals speak Papiamentu, but Dutch and English are also widely understood. A few friendly phrases in Papiamentu—like "Bon dia" (Good morning)—can go a long way.

Power Outlets: Bonaire uses the same voltage (127V) and plug types as the U.S., so no adapters are needed for most visitors. European travelers may need a converter.

Transportation: Renting a car is the best way to explore Bonaire. Taxis are available but can be expensive, and public transport is limited.

Eco-Friendly Behavior: Bonaire is serious about conservation. Avoid single-use plastics, don't touch the coral, and follow all local guidelines to protect the island's natural beauty.

By keeping these tips in mind, you'll be well-prepared for your trip. With your documents in order and a little planning, you can focus on enjoying everything Bonaire has to offer!

Getting to Bonaire: Flights and Transportation

Reaching Bonaire is relatively straightforward, and whether you're flying directly or connecting through a nearby hub, the journey is worth it. Here's what you need to know about getting to this Caribbean gem.

Flights to Bonaire

Bonaire is served by Flamingo International Airport (BON), a small but efficient airport located just outside the capital, Kralendijk. While it doesn't handle the volume of larger Caribbean airports, it offers several convenient options for travelers.

From the U.S.: Direct flights to Bonaire are available from major cities like Miami (American Airlines) and Atlanta (Delta Air Lines). These routes are typically more frequent during the peak tourist season (December to April).

From Europe: Many European travelers connect through Amsterdam, with KLM and TUI offering direct flights from the Netherlands to Bonaire.

From Nearby Islands: If you're island-hopping, you can fly to Bonaire from Aruba or Curaçao via regional carriers like Divi Divi Air and EZ Air. These short flights are a convenient option if you're combining Bonaire with other destinations in the Caribbean.

It's a good idea to book your flights early, especially if you're traveling during peak season, as seats can fill up quickly.

Airport Transfers: Many hotels and resorts offer airport shuttle services. Check with your lodging to see if this is included. Alternatively, taxis are readily available outside the airport, and fares are generally fixed.

Travel Tips: Many flights to Bonaire are on smaller aircraft, so check your airline's baggage policies, especially if you're traveling with dive equipment.

To reach Bonaire apart from flights, you can travel by **sea**. While it doesn't have a large-scale ferry system connecting it to other islands, there are a few options:

- **Cruise Ships**: Bonaire is a popular stop for many Caribbean cruise lines. If you're on a cruise, you might be able to visit Bonaire as part of your itinerary.
- **Private Boats or Yachts**: Bonaire is a favorite destination for sailors, thanks to its pristine waters and well-equipped marinas. If you're traveling by private yacht or charter boat, you can dock at one of the island's harbors.
- **Cargo or Supply Ships**: Some inter-island cargo ships also allow limited passenger travel, though these services are less common and more basic compared to commercial ferries.

For most travelers, flights are the easiest and quickest option, but arriving by sea adds an adventurous touch to your journey!

No matter how you choose to travel to Bonaire or explore it once you're there, the journey will be part of the adventure. From smooth flights to sea cruise, getting to Bonaire is just the beginning of an unforgettable experience.

3. Getting Around the Island

Transportation options

Now that you've arrived on Bonaire, let's talk about how to get around. While the island is small, having a good plan for transportation will make your trip much easier—and much more enjoyable. Here's a closer look at your options.

Renting a Car: The Most Flexible Choice

For most visitors, renting a car is the way to go. It gives you the freedom to explore Bonaire at your own pace, from its peaceful beaches to its rugged national parks. Whether you're heading to a dive site, a remote hiking trail, or a local restaurant, a car will get you there.

AB Car Rental:
Located in Kralendijk, this company offers vehicles ranging from sedans to pickup trucks perfect for divers. Rates start at $29.50 per day. They also provide $0 liability and $0 deposit options. Website: www.abbonaire.com

Avis Bonaire:
Situated near the airport, Avis offers options like the Hyundai Accent and Jeep Wrangler, with daily rates starting around $75 depending on the vehicle and season. Website: www.avis.com/car-rental/bonaire

Caribe Car Rental:
Caribe Car Rental has a variety of vehicles available and competitive pricing. It's a solid choice for hassle-free travel around the island. Website: www.caribecarrental.com

What to Expect: Rental options include sedans, SUVs, and pickup trucks. If you're a diver, you'll love the trucks—they make hauling gear to shore dive spots a breeze.
Tips: Book your rental in advance, especially if you're visiting during peak season. And don't worry—driving is on the right side of the road, and traffic is light.

Scooters and Bikes: For the Adventurous Traveler

If you're feeling adventurous and don't mind a bit of sun, renting a scooter or bike can be a fun way to get around. It's also a more eco-friendly option if you're sticking to shorter distances.

Scooters: They're a zippy way to explore the island, especially if you're staying close to Kralendijk. Just be cautious on windy days, as the trade winds can be strong.
Bicycles: Perfect for leisurely rides along the coastline or around town. Many places rent sturdy bikes designed for the island's terrain.

AB Scooter Rental:
Offers electric scooters and fat bikes with rates starting at $19 per day. Their rentals include a $0 deductible and $0 deposit. Website: www.abscooterrental.com

Greenbikes Bonaire:
Specializes in electric scooters, making it easy and sustainable to explore the island. Website: www.greenbikesbonaire.com

Smiley Rentals:
Provides 125cc scooters for $55 for 2 days or $22.50 per day for rentals over 3 days. Rentals include third-party liability insurance. Website: www.smileyrentals.com

Considerations:
Always wear a helmet when riding scooters.
Be mindful of the island's strong winds and the Caribbean sun—apply sunscreen and drink plenty of water.

Taxis: Convenient, but Limited

Taxis are available on Bonaire, but they're not as common as you might find in busier tourist destinations. They're a good option for quick trips, like getting from the airport to your hotel or heading out for dinner.

Fares: Taxis don't have meters, so you'll want to agree on the fare before your ride.

Availability: You can usually find taxis at the airport, near major hotels, or by calling ahead.

A Note About Public Transportation

Public transportation is almost non-existent on Bonaire. There are no buses or shared shuttles, so having your own mode of transportation is essential for exploring beyond walking distance.

Which Option is Best for You?
If you plan to visit multiple dive sites, beaches, or natural attractions, a car rental is your best bet.
Staying close to town and only venturing out occasionally? A scooter or bike might be all you need.
For quick and easy point-to-point trips, taxis can fill the gap.

Bonaire's laid-back vibe makes getting around easy and stress-free, no matter which option you choose. With a little planning, you'll be cruising from one breathtaking spot to the next in no time.

Tips for Navigating the Island

Once you've decided how you'll get around, here are some practical tips to make your travel around Bonaire as smooth as possible:

1. Stay on Paved Roads Where Possible
While Bonaire's main roads are in good condition, some routes to beaches, dive sites, or remote areas can be unpaved and bumpy. If you plan to explore off-the-beaten-path locations, consider renting a pickup truck or an SUV with higher ground clearance.

2. Fuel Up Frequently
Gas stations aren't plentiful on the island, so it's a good idea to top up your tank whenever you're near one. Most stations are located in or near Kralendijk, and not all of them accept credit cards, so keep some cash handy just in case.

3. Mind the Speed Limits
Speed limits in Bonaire are generally low, reflecting the island's relaxed pace of life. The maximum speed is usually 60 km/h (37 mph) on major roads and 40 km/h (25 mph) in towns. Watch for road signs, and remember that driving responsibly keeps both locals and wildlife safe.

4. Be Cautious of Wildlife
Goats, donkeys, and iguanas are common on Bonaire and often wander onto the roads. Drive carefully, especially in rural areas, and always be prepared to stop for animals crossing.

5. Use GPS or Maps
Most major navigation apps like Google Maps work well on Bonaire, but having a paper map as a backup can be helpful, especially in areas with limited cell coverage. Many car rental agencies provide maps with popular attractions and dive sites marked.

6. Park Safely
Parking is generally easy and free throughout the island, but avoid blocking access to homes, businesses, or the shorelines. If you're parking near a dive site, don't leave valuables in your vehicle.

7. Drive During the Day
While driving at night is safe, there is limited street lighting on some roads, particularly outside Kralendijk. If you're not familiar with the area, it's easier to navigate during daylight hours.

8. Respect Local Driving Customs
Bonaireans are known for their laid-back attitude, which extends to the roads. Use your horn sparingly, and don't be surprised if drivers wave or stop to let you pass. It's part of the island's friendly culture.

9. Be Prepared for Windy Conditions

Bonaire's trade winds are a constant presence, especially along the coast. If you're biking or riding a scooter, plan your route accordingly and expect some resistance when riding into the wind.

By keeping these tips in mind, you'll be well-prepared to explore Bonaire's natural beauty and hidden gems with ease and confidence. From the vibrant reefs to the serene salt flats, navigating the island is part of the adventure.

4. Diving and Snorkeling in Bonaire

Overview of Bonaire National Marine Park

When it comes to underwater adventures, Bonaire is in a league of its own. Known as a diver's paradise, this Caribbean gem offers some of the most pristine and accessible snorkeling and diving spots in the world. At the heart of it all is the Bonaire National Marine Park—a true treasure for marine enthusiasts.

What is the Bonaire National Marine Park?

The Bonaire National Marine Park isn't just another protected area. It's a global model for marine conservation. Established in 1979, the park surrounds the entire island of Bonaire and Klein Bonaire, covering about 2,700 hectares of coral reefs, seagrass beds, and mangroves. It's like stepping into an underwater Eden.

The park isn't just about pretty fish and coral—it's a living, breathing ecosystem teeming with life. You'll find more than 350 species of fish, 60 types of coral, and countless other marine creatures. And the best part? The waters are so clear, you can often see everything in vivid detail, even from the surface.

The park is managed by STINAPA (Stichting Nationale Parken Bonaire), a non-profit foundation dedicated to protecting Bonaire's natural resources. They focus on education, sustainable tourism, and marine conservation.

Bonaire National Marine Park is a testament to how responsible tourism and environmental stewardship can coexist. It offers a unique experience for nature lovers while emphasizing the importance of protecting our planet's delicate ecosystems.

Why is the Marine Park Special?

What makes this park truly unique is the island's commitment to keeping it pristine. Bonaire has been a pioneer in marine conservation. Since the early days, the island has enforced strict rules to protect its reefs. For example:

Mandatory Nature Fee: Before diving or snorkeling, you'll need to purchase a nature tag. The funds go directly to conservation efforts. As of now, it's $40 for divers and $20 for other water activities.

No Touching Rule: Divers and snorkelers are reminded to keep their hands off the coral—these ecosystems are delicate and take decades to grow.

Mooring System: Instead of anchoring boats, the park uses a system of mooring buoys to prevent anchor damage to the reefs.

These measures have paid off, making Bonaire one of the best-preserved marine environments in the Caribbean.

Easy Access for Everyone

One of the most exciting things about Bonaire's marine park is how accessible it is. You don't need a boat to experience world-class diving or snorkeling. Many sites are just steps from the shore, making it easy to grab your gear and jump in.

Whether you're an experienced diver exploring deeper reefs or a beginner sticking to the shallows, there's something for everyone. You'll feel like you're swimming in a giant aquarium, surrounded by colorful fish, graceful turtles, and vibrant coral gardens.

Steps to Visit Bonaire National Marine Park

The park is accessible from virtually anywhere on the island since it includes the surrounding waters. Most accommodations, dive shops, and tour operators on Bonaire are closely connected to the park.

Purchase a Nature Fee (Marine Park Tag):
To enter the park or engage in activities like snorkeling, diving, or kayaking, you must buy a **STINAPA Nature Fee**.
Cost: Typically around $40–$50 for divers and $20 for other water activities (subject to change). Where to buy:

- Dive shops
- STINAPA Bonaire offices
- Online at **https://stinapabonaire.org**.

Choose Your Activity and Location:
- Shore Access: Many dive and snorkel sites are accessible from the shore. Popular spots include **1000 Steps**, **Salt Pier**, and **Lac Bay**.
- Boat Tours: For locations farther offshore, such as Klein Bonaire, book a boat trip or a water taxi from the main harbor in **Kralendijk** (Bonaire's capital).
- Rent Gear or Join a Guided Tour: If you're snorkeling or diving, rent gear from the numerous dive shops on the island.

Joining a guided tour is an excellent option if you're new to marine exploration or want to visit specific sites like the mangroves.

Visit Klein Bonaire: Take a water taxi from Kralendijk to this uninhabited islet (part of the marine park). The ride takes 15–20 minutes, and the snorkeling around Klein Bonaire is world-class.

Explore the Mangroves: Head to **Lac Bay** or **Mangrove Center Bonaire**, where you can kayak or take an eco-tour of the mangroves. These tours often include fascinating insights into the marine park's ecosystem.

Guided Tours to consider

Bonaire offers a variety of guided tours tailored for beginners interested in snorkeling and scuba diving. Here are some reputable options to consider:

Woodwind Snorkel Tours: If you're new to snorkeling, this is an excellent choice. Woodwind offers guided tours around **Klein Bonaire**, complete with high-quality gear

and expert guidance. They cater specifically to beginners, explaining marine life along the way. Plus, their tours often include a delicious lunch or snacks on the boat.
Contact: info@woodwindbonaire.com | +599 786 7055

Seacow Snorkel Trips:
Seacow is famous for its small, friendly group tours. The guides take you to two of Bonaire's best snorkeling spots and provide personal attention to ensure you feel confident in the water. Beginners love their laid-back vibe and thorough instructions before diving into the crystal-clear waters.
Contact: info@seacow-bonaire.com | +599 780 5353

Dive Friends Bonaire – Discover Scuba Diving:
Want to try scuba diving but have zero experience? Dive Friends Bonaire's **Discover Scuba Diving** program is perfect for first-timers. You'll learn the basics and have your first dive in a calm, shallow area under the supervision of patient and professional instructors.
Contact: info@divefriendsbonaire.com | +599 717 2929

Dive Diva Bonaire:
This is a boutique diving experience. Dive Diva is ideal for those who want private, personalized attention. Whether you're snorkeling or diving for the first time, they'll customize the experience to your comfort level. Perfect if you're feeling a little nervous!
Contact: info@divedivabonaire.com | +599 795 1130

H2O Visions Bonaire:
H2O Visions specializes in beginner-friendly snorkeling and eco-tours. Their guides are incredibly knowledgeable and will teach you everything you need to know about the marine ecosystem. They keep the groups small, so you'll get plenty of help and attention.
Contact: info@h2ovisionsbonaire.com | +599 780 7237

These tours not only guide you through the basics of snorkeling or diving but also ensure you come away with unforgettable memories of Bonaire's breathtaking underwater world.

The Bonaire National Marine Park isn't just a destination—it's an experience that stays with you long after you leave the island. Whether you're diving deep or floating on the surface, you're part of something truly special here.

Top Dive and Snorkel Sites

Bonaire's underwater world is a playground for divers and snorkelers, with over 80 marked dive sites around the island and Klein Bonaire. The calm, crystal-clear waters and vibrant marine life make every site a memorable experience. Here are some of the top spots to add to your list:

Hilma Hooker

Type: Wreck Dive
Depth: 60-100 feet (18-30 meters)

The Hilma Hooker is Bonaire's most famous wreck dive. This 236-foot cargo ship sits on its side, providing an incredible habitat for marine life like barracudas, tarpons, and colorful corals. The wreck is accessible to advanced divers, but even beginners can explore the shallower parts.

1000 Steps

Type: Shore Dive/Snorkel
Depth: 20-100 feet (6-30 meters)

Don't let the name scare you—it's actually only about 70 steps down to the beach. This iconic site is known for its beautiful coral formations, sea turtles, and abundant fish species. It's great for both snorkeling and diving, with easy access from the shore.

Klein Bonaire

Type: Boat Dive/Snorkel
Depth: Varies

Klein Bonaire, the uninhabited islet off Bonaire's coast, is a treasure trove of dive and snorkel sites. No Name Beach is a popular spot, perfect for snorkeling and spotting turtles in the shallows. Boat operators offer easy trips to Klein Bonaire, making it accessible for all skill levels.

Salt Pier

Type: Shore Dive
Depth: 15-50 feet (5-15 meters)

Diving under the Salt Pier is like stepping into an underwater art gallery. The towering pillars are covered in vibrant sponges and corals, and schools of fish swirl around them. This site is especially photogenic, and you might even spot eagle rays or octopuses.

Bari Reef
Type: Shore Dive/Snorkel
Depth: 20-100 feet (6-30 meters)

If you're a fan of biodiversity, Bari Reef is a must. Known as one of the most species-rich reefs in the Caribbean, this site is teeming with marine life, from small reef fish to moray eels and even seahorses. It's an excellent choice for beginner snorkelers and divers.

Buddy Dive Reef

Type: Shore Dive
Depth: 20-100 feet (6-30 meters)

Located right off Buddy Dive Resort, this house reef is perfect for a convenient and rewarding dive. It's a great spot for night diving, where you can see the reef come alive with nocturnal creatures like lobsters and shrimp.

Lac Bay

Type: Snorkel
Depth: Shallow

For a relaxing snorkel experience, head to Lac Bay on the eastern side of the island. The calm, shallow waters are ideal for spotting rays, conch, and even baby sharks. Mangroves nearby also provide a unique habitat worth exploring.

Andrea I and Andrea II
Depth: 20-100 feet (6-30 meters)

These twin sites offer stunning coral formations and plenty of marine life. They're accessible from the shore and less crowded than some of the more famous spots, making them a peaceful option for exploring the underwater world.

Karpata
Type: Shore Dive
Depth: 20-100 feet (6-30 meters)

Karpata offers dramatic coral formations and an abundance of marine life, including groupers, angelfish, and the occasional sea turtle. The drive to this site is scenic, adding to the overall experience.

Alice in Wonderland
Type: Shore Dive/Snorkel
Depth: 20-100 feet (6-30 meters)

Type: Shore Dive/Snorkel

This site lives up to its name, with colorful coral gardens that feel like a dream world. It's a favorite among snorkelers and divers alike for its vibrant reefs and calm conditions.

Tips for Visiting Dive and Snorkel Sites
Bring Reef-Safe Sunscreen: Protect the coral by using eco-friendly sunscreen.
Pack Gear or Rent Locally: Many dive shops on the island offer high-quality gear for rent.
Dive with a Buddy: Safety first—always dive or snorkel with a partner.
Respect Marine Life: Observe creatures from a distance, and never touch the coral.

Bonaire's underwater world is as breathtaking as its land-based scenery. With so many incredible spots to choose from, every dive or snorkel promises a new adventure.

If you're planning to dive or snorkel in Bonaire, you won't need to lug heavy gear with you. The island is well-equipped with dive shops, rental facilities, and professional guides ready to make your underwater adventure seamless and memorable.

Gear Rental

Most dive shops on Bonaire offer high-quality rental equipment, including masks, fins, wetsuits, BCDs, and tanks. Here are a few popular options:

Dive Friends Bonaire:
With multiple locations around the island, Dive Friends offers a full range of rental gear at competitive prices. Tank rentals start at $12, and complete dive sets are available for around $35 per day. Their convenient pick-up and drop-off system makes it easy to gear up for a day of diving.
Website: www.divefriendsbonaire.com

Buddy Dive Resort:
Renowned for its exceptional facilities, Buddy Dive rents top-notch gear and provides unlimited air or nitrox tank packages starting at $185 per week. Their house reef is also a great spot to test your equipment before heading out.
Website: www.buddydive.com

VIP Diving:
VIP Diving focuses on personalized service and high-end gear. They cater to small groups, making it ideal for those who prefer a tailored experience. Daily rentals start at $45 for a complete set.
Website: www.vipdiving.com

Dive Shops

Dive shops on Bonaire aren't just about rentals—they're hubs for tips, dive maps, and local expertise. Many also offer courses, certifications, and workshops for all skill levels.

Wannadive Bonaire:
Known for its laid-back atmosphere, Wannadive provides detailed dive site maps and rental gear. Their unlimited air packages start at $140 per week.
Website: www.wannadive.com

Captain Don's Habitat:
A pioneer in sustainable diving, Captain Don's is a full-service dive shop with eco-friendly practices. They also organize guided night dives and underwater photography tours.
Website: www.habitatbonaire.com

Guided Tours

For those who prefer to have a local expert by their side, guided dive and snorkel tours are a fantastic option.
Dive Friends Bonaire:
Offers guided shore dives starting at $45 per person. Their guides are knowledgeable about marine life and can help you navigate some of the more challenging dive sites.

Sea Turtle Conservation Bonaire:
If you want a purposeful dive, join a sea turtle tagging and monitoring trip. These tours combine diving with marine conservation efforts.
Website: www.bonaireturtles.org

Woodwind Snorkel & Sailing:
Perfect for snorkelers, Woodwind offers half-day sailing tours to Klein Bonaire, complete with equipment, snacks, and knowledgeable guides. Rates start at $75 per person.
Website: www.woodwindbonaire.com

Tips for Renting Gear and Booking Tours

Book in Advance: During peak season, rental gear and guided tours can fill up quickly. Reserve early to secure your spot.

Inspect Your Gear: Before heading out, double-check that your equipment fits properly and functions correctly.

Ask for Local Advice: Dive shop staff often have insider tips on the best sites based on current conditions.

Consider Insurance: Some shops offer optional damage insurance for rental gear—worth considering if you're diving frequently.

Whether you're a seasoned diver or a first-time snorkeler, Bonaire's dive shops and tour operators make it easy to explore the island's stunning underwater world. With the right gear and guidance, all you need to do is dive in and enjoy!

5. Outdoor Adventures Beyond Diving

Windsurfing at Lac Bay

While Bonaire is world-famous for its diving, the island offers so much more for those who love the outdoors. If you're looking for thrills above the waves, windsurfing at Lac Bay is an absolute must.

Lac Bay, located on Bonaire's east coast, is a slice of paradise for windsurfing enthusiasts. The bay's shallow, warm waters and steady trade winds create perfect conditions for riders of all levels. Whether you're a seasoned windsurfer or a complete beginner, Lac Bay has something for everyone.

Why Lac Bay is Perfect for Windsurfing
The bay is protected by a coral reef, keeping the waters calm even as the winds pick up. This makes it ideal for practicing your balance and trying out new tricks without worrying about big waves. Plus, the scenery is stunning—you'll glide across turquoise waters surrounded by mangroves and pristine beaches.

Where to Go
Two popular windsurfing schools operate at Lac Bay:

Jibe City
Known for its friendly vibe and excellent instructors, Jibe City is a go-to spot for both lessons and rentals. Beginner lessons start at around $60 per hour, and gear rental ranges from $25 to $75, depending on the duration and equipment type. After a session on the water, relax at their beach bar, The Hang Out, which serves refreshing drinks and snacks. Website: www.jibecity.com

The Windsurf Place
This family-owned center caters to all skill levels with a range of rental equipment and lessons. Their instructors are patient and great at helping beginners build confidence on the board. Rates are similar to Jibe City, and they also offer packages for multi-day rentals or lessons. Website: www.windsurfplace.com

What to Expect
If you're new to windsurfing, don't worry—the learning curve is surprisingly quick. Within an hour, most beginners can stand up and start gliding across the water. For experienced windsurfers, the bay offers plenty of space to pick up speed and test out advanced moves.

Tips for Windsurfing at Lac Bay
Wear Reef-Safe Sunscreen: The sun can be intense, and you'll want to protect both your skin and the environment.
Book Lessons in Advance: Lac Bay is a popular spot, especially during peak seasons, so it's wise to secure your lesson or gear rental early.

Bring Water Shoes: The sandy bottom of the bay can be a bit rocky in some areas, so water shoes can be helpful.

Stay Hydrated: It's easy to lose track of time when you're having fun in the sun, so keep a water bottle handy.

Windsurfing at Lac Bay isn't just a sport—it's an experience that captures the free-spirited energy of Bonaire. Whether you're zipping across the water or simply soaking in the views, it's a day well spent in paradise.

Kiteboarding Hotspots

If you're looking for an adrenaline rush on the water, kiteboarding in Bonaire is an experience like no other. The island's consistent trade winds, warm waters, and dedicated kiteboarding spots make it a top destination for this thrilling sport.

Where to Kiteboard in Bonaire

The main kiteboarding action happens on the island's southwest coast, where conditions are ideal for riders of all levels. Here's where to go:

Atlantis Kite Beach
Atlantis Kite Beach, located near the southern tip of Bonaire, is the island's premier kiteboarding spot. The steady onshore winds and wide-open spaces make it a favorite for both beginners and experienced riders. The area has a sandy entry point, and the deep water ensures safe landings for jumps and tricks.

What to Expect:
The wind at Atlantis Kite Beach averages between 15 and 25 knots year-round, providing consistent conditions. The beach itself is remote and peaceful, so you can focus entirely on riding the waves or mastering your skills.

Klein Bonaire
For those who want a more secluded experience, the waters around Klein Bonaire offer excellent kiteboarding opportunities. You'll need a boat to reach the islet, but the effort is rewarded with flat, crystal-clear waters perfect for freestyle riding.

Kiteboarding Schools and Rentals

Bonaire has several kiteboarding schools that cater to all skill levels. Here are the top ones to check out:

Kiteboarding Bonaire:
This school, located at Atlantis Kite Beach, is one of the most well-known on the island. They offer lessons for beginners starting at $110 for a one-hour session and package deals for more intensive training. Advanced riders can rent gear starting at $85 per day. Their instructors are IKO-certified, ensuring a safe and professional experience. Website: www.kiteboardingbonaire.com

Wind Bonaire:
Based in Kralendijk, Wind Bonaire provides boat access to kiteboarding spots, including Klein Bonaire. They specialize in small group lessons and offer high-quality rental equipment. Prices start at $100 per hour for lessons. Website: www.windbonaire.com

Bonaire Kite School:

This school prides itself on personalized instruction with a focus on safety. Their lessons start at $120 per hour, and they also offer tandem rides for those who want to experience kiteboarding without taking the reins. Website: www.bonairekiteschool.com

Tips for Kiteboarding in Bonaire

Wind Conditions: Bonaire's winds are strongest from December to August, making these months the best time for kiteboarding.

Safety First: Beginners should always take lessons before heading out on their own. Kiteboarding can be challenging, but proper instruction makes a big difference.

Wear Sun Protection: A rash guard and reef-safe sunscreen are essential to protect your skin from the intense Caribbean sun.

Respect the Environment: Bonaire is known for its pristine waters and marine life. Be mindful of where you launch and ride to avoid damaging coral reefs or disturbing wildlife.

Whether you're new to the sport or an experienced kiteboarder, Bonaire's kiteboarding scene offers the perfect blend of adventure and natural beauty. With consistent winds and world-class instruction, you'll be riding the waves in no time.

While windsurfing and kiteboarding bring excitement to Bonaire's coastline, the island's natural beauty extends far beyond the water. For those looking to connect with nature in a more tranquil way—or even go on an underground adventure—Bonaire has plenty to offer.

Kayaking Through Mangroves and Calm Waters

Kayaking is a fantastic way to explore Bonaire's diverse ecosystems, especially the mangroves of Lac Bay. This protected area is a haven for wildlife and one of the island's most unique natural wonders. Paddling through the narrow channels feels like entering a hidden world, where birds, fish, and even juvenile sea turtles make their home.

Mangrove Kayak Tours:
Companies like Mangrove Center Bonaire offer guided eco-tours starting at $50 per person. Their knowledgeable guides will explain the mangroves' role in Bonaire's environment and help you spot wildlife you might miss on your own.
Website: www.mangrovecenter.com

Other Kayaking Spots:
For calm, open-water kayaking, head to **Sorobon Beach** or **the coastlines near Klein Bonaire**. Some rental shops provide clear-bottom kayaks, letting you see the underwater world as you paddle.

Hiking Trails With Stunning Views

Bonaire's dry, rugged terrain is perfect for hiking, with trails that take you through dramatic landscapes and offer breathtaking views.

Washington Slagbaai National Park:

This expansive park in the north is a hiker's paradise. Trails range from easy walks to challenging climbs, such as the Brandaris Hill Trail. At 784 feet, Brandaris is the highest point on the island, and reaching the summit rewards you with panoramic views of Bonaire and even Curaçao on a clear day. Entry to the park costs $45, which includes access to the Bonaire National Marine Park.

Karpata to Rincon Trail:
This trail takes you through old plantation land and cactus-filled landscapes, giving you a glimpse of Bonaire's history and natural beauty. It's a great choice for those who want a mix of culture and outdoor adventure.

Lac Cai Nature Walks:
If you prefer something more low-key, Lac Cai offers shorter trails where you can stroll along sandy paths and watch flamingos feed in the shallow waters.

Caving Adventures

Bonaire's caves are a hidden treasure for thrill-seekers and nature lovers alike. Over 400 caves are scattered across the island, with many open for exploration. Some are dry caves adorned with ancient stalactites and stalagmites, while others are "wet caves" featuring crystal-clear pools perfect for swimming.

Cave Tours:
Guided tours are highly recommended for safety and to learn about the caves' fascinating history and geology. Flow Bonaire offers tours starting at $55 per person, including all necessary equipment and expert guidance.
Website: www.flowbonaire.com

Popular Caves to Explore:
Barcadera Cave: Known for its dramatic formations and historical significance.
Lac Cai Caves: These wet caves are ideal for a refreshing swim and a unique underground experience.
Spelonk Lighthouse Caves: Located near the eastern coastline, these caves offer a more remote and adventurous outing.

Tips for Outdoor Adventures
Stay Hydrated: Bonaire's climate is hot and dry, so bring plenty of water, especially for hiking.

Wear Proper Footwear: Trails can be rocky, so sturdy shoes are essential for hiking and caving.

Book in Advance: Tours for kayaking and caving can fill up quickly, particularly in peak season. Respect the Environment: Leave no trace, and avoid touching sensitive formations in the caves.

From serene kayaking trips through mangroves to climbing Bonaire's highest peak and venturing into mysterious caves, the island offers something for every type of adventurer. These activities are the perfect way to balance your water-based fun with unforgettable land-based experiences.

6. Exploring Bonaire's Natural Wonders

Washington Slagbaai National Park

While the ocean may steal the spotlight in Bonaire, the island's rugged terrain and incredible biodiversity deserve just as much attention. For anyone seeking to connect with nature, a visit to Washington Slagbaai National Park is a must. This sprawling park offers a mix of stunning landscapes, unique wildlife, and a glimpse into Bonaire's history.

Located in the northern part of the island, Washington Slagbaai National Park is a massive nature reserve that spans over 13,500 acres. It's a haven for hikers, birdwatchers, and anyone who loves wide-open spaces. The park was established in 1969, making it the first nature sanctuary in the Dutch Caribbean.

What makes the park special is its variety. You'll find cacti-covered hills, salt flats, mangroves, and hidden beaches—all in one place. It's also home to Bonaire's highest peak, Brandaris Hill, and an abundance of wildlife, including flamingos, iguanas, and native parrots.

What to Do in the Park

Hiking:
The park offers several trails for all fitness levels. The most popular hike is to the top of Brandaris Hill. At 784 feet, it's the highest point on the island, and the views from the summit are breathtaking. You can see the turquoise waters surrounding Bonaire and even spot Curaçao on a clear day.

Scenic Drives:
If hiking isn't your thing, you can explore the park by car. There are two driving routes:
- The short route takes about two hours and is perfect for a quick visit.
- The long route takes four hours and covers more of the park, including some secluded beaches.

Both routes are unpaved and can be bumpy, so a 4x4 or sturdy vehicle is recommended.

Wildlife Watching:
The park is a birdwatcher's paradise. Flamingos flock to the salt flats, and you'll likely hear the chatter of yellow-shouldered parrots. Keep an eye out for iguanas basking in the sun and small goats wandering through the cacti.

Beaches:
The park is home to a few pristine beaches, such as Playa Chikitu and Boka Kokolishi. These spots are perfect for a peaceful picnic or a chance to admire the crashing waves. Swimming is limited due to rough currents, but the views alone are worth the visit.

History of the Park

The land that now makes up Washington Slagbaai National Park was once two plantations: Washington and Slagbaai. These plantations were crucial to Bonaire's economy, producing salt, aloe, and charcoal for export. Today, remnants of this history can still be seen in the old buildings scattered throughout the park.

Visitor Information

- Entrance Fee: Entry costs $45 per person, which also includes access to the Bonaire National Marine Park. If you're only visiting the park, a standalone ticket is $20.
- Hours: The park is open daily from 8:00 AM to 5:00 PM, but the last entrance is at 2:45 PM to ensure visitors have enough time to explore before closing.

What to Bring:

- Plenty of water and snacks—there are no shops inside the park.
- Sun protection, such as a hat and reef-safe sunscreen.
- Sturdy shoes for hiking.
- Binoculars if you're interested in birdwatching.

Tips for Visiting the Park

Start Early: Bonaire's sun can be intense, so it's best to visit in the morning when temperatures are cooler.

Plan for the Terrain: The unpaved roads can be rough, so make sure your vehicle is up for the challenge.

Respect Wildlife: Keep a safe distance from animals, and don't feed them—it's important to maintain the natural balance of the park.

Washington Slagbaai National Park is more than just a day trip; it's an immersion into Bonaire's wild side. Whether you're hiking to Brandaris, spotting flamingos, or simply soaking up the views, the park is a reminder of how untouched and beautiful nature can be.

Flamingo Sanctuary and Salt Flats

Bonaire's landscapes are as diverse as they are stunning, and the flamingo sanctuary and salt flats are a prime example. These areas showcase the island's natural beauty while offering a chance to observe its most famous residents—the graceful pink flamingos.

The Flamingo Sanctuary

Located near Gotomeer Lake in the north and in the salt flats of the south, Bonaire's flamingo sanctuaries are a must-see for wildlife enthusiasts. These spots are critical breeding grounds for the Caribbean flamingo, one of the largest flamingo species in the world. With their vibrant plumage and elegant movements, they're a sight to behold.

Gotomeer Lake:
This saltwater lagoon is surrounded by hills and cacti, creating a picturesque setting. Flamingos flock here to feed on brine shrimp, a primary food source that gives them their iconic pink color. Early mornings and late afternoons are the best times to visit, as the flamingos are more active then.

Pekelmeer Flamingo Sanctuary:
Situated near Bonaire's southern salt flats, this sanctuary is one of only four breeding grounds for flamingos in the entire Caribbean. It's a protected area, so you can't walk through it, but you can observe the flamingos from a distance.

Salt Flats: A Unique Landscape

Bonaire's salt flats are not only an important part of the island's economy but also a fascinating natural wonder. The flats, located in the southern region near Pekelmeer, are used for salt production, a practice that dates back to the 17th century.

The salt pans are shallow pools that reflect the sky, creating a surreal, mirror-like effect. Depending on the light and time of day, the pools can appear pink or even purple, thanks to the microorganisms that thrive in the brine. Towering white salt pyramids nearby add to the otherworldly atmosphere.

The Process:
Saltwater is pumped into the flats and allowed to evaporate, leaving behind raw sea salt. The salt is then harvested and exported, with some of it even used for Bonaire's local dishes.

Why Visit the Salt Flats?
The striking visuals of the salt flats make them a photographer's dream. They're also a great spot for learning about Bonaire's history and how salt production shaped its economy.

Tips for Visiting Flamingo and Salt Flat Areas

Bring Binoculars: To get a closer look at the flamingos without disturbing them.

Plan Around the Sun: The light during sunrise or sunset makes the salt flats particularly stunning for photography.

Respect the Sanctuaries: Stay on designated paths and avoid getting too close to the flamingos to protect their natural habitat.

Combine Visits: Pair a trip to the salt flats with a stop at nearby beaches like Sorobon or Pink Beach to make the most of your day.

Between the delicate beauty of the flamingos and the striking scenery of the salt flats, this part of Bonaire offers a tranquil yet awe-inspiring experience. It's a chance to slow down and take in the quieter side of the island's natural wonders.

Beaches, Mangroves, and Hidden Coves

onaire's coastline is a blend of serene beaches, vibrant mangroves, and secluded coves, each offering its own charm and unique experience. Whether you're seeking relaxation, wildlife encounters, or a touch of adventure, this island's natural beauty has something for everyone.

Beaches: Relaxation and Beauty

Bonaire isn't known for sprawling sandy beaches like some Caribbean islands, but its shores are no less captivating. Here are some standout spots:

Sorobon Beach:
Located on the eastern side of the island, Sorobon Beach is a favorite for its shallow, calm waters. It's perfect for families, beginners trying their hand at windsurfing, or anyone looking to wade into turquoise waters. Local beach bars like The Hangout Beach Bar make it a great spot to spend the day.

Pink Beach:
Named for the faint pink hue of its sands, this beach offers a quiet escape. It's ideal for snorkeling, sunbathing, or enjoying a picnic with a view of the crystal-clear water.

Te Amo Beac:
Conveniently close to the airport, this beach is a hit with locals and visitors alike. The snorkeling here is excellent, and food trucks nearby often serve up tasty local dishes.

Mangroves: A Vital Ecosystem

Bonaire's mangroves are more than just picturesque—they're an essential part of the island's ecosystem. These dense, tree-filled wetlands provide a sanctuary for fish, birds, and even juvenile sea turtles.

Lac Bay Mangroves
The mangroves at Lac Bay are a magical place to explore by kayak or paddleboard. As you glide through the narrow channels, you'll feel like you've stepped into another world. Guided eco-tours, such as those offered by Mangrove Center Bonaire (www.mangrovecenter.com, tours start at $50), are a fantastic way to learn about this unique habitat while experiencing its tranquility.

Why Visit the Mangroves?
Beyond their beauty, the mangroves play a crucial role in protecting Bonaire's coastline from erosion and serving as a nursery for marine life. Visiting them offers both insight and inspiration.

Hidden Coves: Seclusion and Adventure

For those who love a bit of exploration, Bonaire's hidden coves provide a more secluded experience. These lesser-known spots are perfect for adventurous travelers looking to escape the crowds.

Boka Kokolishi
Tucked within Washington Slagbaai National Park, this cove is known for its dramatic rock formations and natural pools. While swimming isn't always safe due to strong currents, it's a stunning place to relax and take in the scenery.

1,000 Steps
Despite its intimidating name, this site only has about 60 steps leading down to a small, pebbly beach. Popular among snorkelers and divers, it

offers incredible underwater views and a peaceful setting.

Boka Slagbaai

Another gem within the national park, this cove is a great place for swimming and spotting wildlife. It's quieter than many beaches, making it an excellent choice for those seeking solitude.

Tips for Exploring Bonaire's Coastal Gems

Pack Smart: Bring reef-safe sunscreen, water shoes, and snorkeling gear for the best experience.

Timing Matters: Visit early in the morning or late in the afternoon to avoid crowds and heat.

Stay Safe: Pay attention to signage about currents, especially at secluded coves.

Leave No Trace: Help preserve Bonaire's beauty by taking all trash with you and respecting its natural environment.

From soft sandy beaches to lush mangroves and tucked-away coves, Bonaire's coastline offers endless opportunities to relax, explore, and connect with nature. Each spot has its own story and character, making them well worth discovering.

We'd Love to Hear From You

Are you enjoying this travel guide? Your thoughts and feedback are incredibly valuable to us. We want to make sure this book truly enhances your journey and provides the insights you're looking for.

If you have a moment, we'd be so grateful if you could share your honest feedback. It's easy—just scan the QR code to leave your feedback. Your input not only helps us improve but also guides other travelers like you.

Thank you for being a part of this adventure and for helping us make future editions even better!

Highlights of Bonaire's colorful capital

Bonaire's capital, Kralendijk, might be small, but it's packed with personality. This charming seaside town is the heart of the island, where pastel-colored buildings, a laid-back vibe, and a touch of history come together to create a memorable experience.

A Walk Through Kralendijk

Strolling through the streets of Kralendijk feels like stepping into a postcard. The town's Dutch colonial architecture is impossible to miss, with buildings painted in bright hues of yellow, blue, and pink. These vibrant colors, paired with the clear blue waters of the Caribbean, set the perfect backdrop for exploring.

Wilhelmina Park
Start your visit at Wilhelmina Park, a peaceful waterfront spot with shady trees and benches. It's a great place to relax, watch the boats in the harbor, and even catch sight of Bonaire's resident iguanas.

Kaya Grandi
This is Kralendijk's main shopping street, lined with boutique stores, souvenir shops, and local craft vendors. You'll find everything from handmade jewelry to locally produced sea salt here. Be sure to browse the markets for one-of-a-kind treasures to take home.

Local Landmarks

Kralendijk may be laid-back, but it's full of little surprises. Here are some spots to check out:

Fort Oranje
Dating back to 1639, Fort Oranje is a historic landmark overlooking the harbor. While the fort is no longer in use, its sturdy walls and iconic lighthouse are a reminder of Bonaire's colonial past.

Terramar Museum
If you're curious about Bonaire's history, the Terramar Museum is the place to go. Located in a beautifully restored building, the museum features exhibits on the island's culture, maritime history, and the

lives of its indigenous people. Entry costs about $10, and it's worth every penny for the insights it offers.

Dining and Drinking in Kralendijk

Kralendijk is also the culinary hub of Bonaire, offering a variety of restaurants and cafes that cater to all tastes.

Local Eats: Try some traditional Caribbean dishes at places like Plaza Senor Coconut or Mi Banana, where fresh fish, goat stew, and funchi (a cornmeal dish) are staples.

Seafood Delights: Being a coastal town, Kralendijk has plenty of options for seafood lovers. Head to It Rains Fishes or Blue Garden Brazilian Grill for a memorable meal with a view.

Laid-Back Cafes: For a casual bite, check out Zazu Bar or grab a coffee and dessert at Gio's Gelateria.

Nightlife and Evening Strolls

When the sun sets, Kralendijk transforms into a lively yet relaxed place. Bars like Karel's Beach Bar, perched over the water, are perfect for sipping cocktails as you watch the horizon fade into twilight. If you prefer something quieter, an evening walk along the waterfront promenade is equally enchanting.

Tips for Visiting Kralendijk

Take Your Time: Kralendijk is best enjoyed at a leisurely pace. Stop often to take in the sights, chat with locals, or simply enjoy the atmosphere.

Support Local: Shop at locally owned stores and dine at family-run restaurants to contribute to the island's economy.

Stay Comfortable: Wear comfortable shoes for walking and bring a hat or sunscreen, as the sun can be intense during the day.

Kralendijk may not be a bustling metropolis, but that's precisely its charm. It's a place to slow down, enjoy simple pleasures, and soak up the friendly, welcoming spirit of Bonaire.

Kralendijk is a treasure trove for shoppers who love unique finds and handcrafted items. From quaint boutiques to vibrant local markets, there's something for everyone. It's the perfect place to pick up a piece of Bonaire to take home.

Shopping Highlights

Kaya Grandi
The main shopping street in Kralendijk, Kaya Grandi, is lined with colorful stores offering everything from high-end jewelry to casual souvenirs. You'll find a mix of international brands and locally owned shops, making it easy to discover a keepsake that suits your style.

Elements Bonaire
Located on Kaya Grandi, this boutique features handmade jewelry and accessories crafted from natural materials like sea glass, driftwood, and semi-precious stones. Each piece is inspired by the island's natural beauty and makes for a meaningful gift or souvenir.

Salt Shop Bonaire
Bonaire is famous for its salt production, and this shop celebrates that heritage. You can pick up gourmet sea salt, bath salts, and even salt scrubs, all locally made. These items make thoughtful, authentic gifts for loved ones back home.

Local Markets

For a more authentic and lively shopping experience, head to one of Kralendijk's markets:

Marshe di Playa
This open-air market, located near the waterfront, is a great spot to browse local produce, handmade crafts, and fresh fish. Vendors often sell one-of-a-kind items like woven baskets, wooden carvings, and embroidered fabrics.

Craft Market at Wilhelmina Park
Every week, local artisans gather in Wilhelmina Park to sell their creations. You'll find everything from paintings and pottery to handmade jewelry. It's a wonderful way to support Bonaire's artists and bring home a piece of the island's culture.

Unique Finds and Local Crafts

Sea Salt Products: Bonaire's salt flats are world-famous, and you'll find many products made from the island's sea salt. In addition to culinary salts, you can purchase bath salts, scrubs, and candles infused with local scents.

Divi Divi Wood Carvings: The divi divi tree, iconic to the Caribbean, inspires local artisans who carve its wood into beautiful decorative pieces. From small figurines to larger sculptures, these make for stunning souvenirs.

Lacquered Shell Jewelry: Local jewelers often incorporate shells and other marine elements into their designs. Lacquered shell necklaces, bracelets, and earrings are popular and reflect Bonaire's coastal charm.

Tips for Shopping in Kralendijk

Bargain a Little: At markets, some light haggling is acceptable, but always be respectful.

Bring Cash: While many shops accept cards, smaller vendors at markets often prefer cash, especially USD or local currency (ANG).

Ask About the Backstory: Many artisans are happy to share the story behind their creations, adding a personal touch to your purchase.

Whether you're browsing high-end boutiques or chatting with vendors at a market stall, shopping in Kralendijk offers more than just souvenirs—it's a chance to connect with Bonaire's creative spirit and take a piece of its charm home with you.

Dining and Nightlife Options

Kralendijk might be small, but it delivers big when it comes to food and evening entertainment. The town's dining scene reflects Bonaire's multicultural influences, from Caribbean and Dutch flavors to international cuisine. As the sun sets, Kralendijk takes on a relaxed but lively energy, with cozy bars and waterfront spots perfect for unwinding.

Where to Eat: Top Dining Spots in Kralendijk

It Rains Fishes

This waterfront restaurant is a favorite for fresh seafood and stunning views. Whether you're in the mood for local fish like wahoo and mahi-mahi or want to try the tuna tataki, everything here is beautifully presented. Mains start around $20-$30, making it a great spot for a special dinner.
Contact: +599 717 8780
Website: itrainsfishesbonaire.com

La Cantina Cervecería

Located in the heart of town, La Cantina offers excellent craft beers, fresh seafood, and flavorful tapas. Their lionfish burger is a standout—tasty, sustainable, and unique to Bonaire. Pair it with one of their local brews, and you're set.
Contact: +599 717 3595
Website: lacantinabonaire.com

Mi Banana

A favorite for authentic, home-cooked Caribbean and Latin dishes, Mi Banana is a cozy, no-frills spot where the portions are generous and the prices are friendly. Try the goat stew, fried fish, or plantains for a true taste of the island.
Contact: +599 701 5741

Gio's Gelateria & Caffé

Perfect for a sweet treat, Gio's serves up some of the best gelato on the island. With flavors like passion fruit, coconut, and Nutella, it's hard to choose just one. It's also a great place for coffee or a light snack during the day.
Contact: +599 717 5700

Posada Para Mira

If you're up for a short drive just outside Kralendijk, this restaurant is well worth it. Set on a hilltop, it offers beautiful views of the island along with traditional dishes like iguana soup, conch, and local goat stew.
Contact: +599 717 7316

Nightlife in Kralendijk: Relaxed and Scenic

Bonaire's nightlife is more laid-back than rowdy. In Kralendijk, evenings revolve around good company, ocean views, and a cocktail or two. Here are some popular spots to visit:

Karel's Beach Bar

One of the most iconic bars in town, Karel's is perched on a pier over the water, offering

incredible sunset views. It's a great spot to enjoy a cold beer, cocktails, or even late-night dancing when the DJ takes over. On weekends, the vibe is livelier with both locals and visitors mingling.
Contact: +599 717 8434
Website: karelsbeachbar.com

Little Havana

For music lovers, Little Havana is the go-to spot. This cozy bar offers live music several nights a week, from reggae to rock, making it one of the liveliest evening hangouts on the island.
Contact: +599 701 0801

The Hangout Beach Bar
Technically located at Sorobon Beach, this bar is worth the short trip from Kralendijk. With its chilled-out vibe, live music, and fresh cocktails, it's a fantastic place to relax after a long day of windsurfing or exploring.
Contact: +599 701 0247
Website: thehangoutbeachbar.com

Spice Beach Club
For a blend of relaxation and nightlife, Spice Beach Club is a top choice. By day, it's a trendy beach hangout with lounge chairs and drinks by the water. At night, it transforms into a vibrant spot with DJs, themed parties, and cocktails under the stars.
Contact: +599 717 8066
Website: spicebonaire.com

Dining and Nightlife Tips
Book Ahead: Popular restaurants like It Rains Fishes and La Cantina fill up quickly, so make a reservation if you're dining at peak times.

Try Lionfish: Many restaurants serve lionfish, an invasive species that's delicious and helps protect the reef ecosystem.

Pace Yourself: The nightlife may not be wild, but it's easy to lose track of time under the stars, so take it slow and enjoy the atmosphere.

Dress Comfortably: Bonaire is casual, even in nicer restaurants and bars. Light, breezy clothing and sandals will serve you well.

Dining and nightlife in Kralendijk reflect the island's easygoing personality. Whether you're savoring fresh seafood, enjoying live music, or watching the sun disappear into the horizon with a cocktail in hand, you'll find that Bonaire's charm doesn't fade after dark.

8. Local Culture and Traditions

Papiamentu: The Language of Bonaire

When visiting Bonaire, one of the first things you'll notice is the sound of Papiamentu, a unique and lively language that reflects the island's rich cultural heritage. It's spoken not only in Bonaire but also across Curaçao and Aruba, and it's a big part of daily life here.

What is Papiamentu?
Papiamentu is a Creole language with roots in Portuguese, Spanish, Dutch, African languages, and even some English. It evolved during the colonial era as a way for people from different backgrounds to communicate, and today, it's a point of pride for Bonaireans.

For example, instead of "hello," you might hear someone say "Bon dia" (good morning), "Bon tardi" (good afternoon), or "Bon nochi" (good night). It's warm and welcoming, much like the people of Bonaire.

A Few Useful Phrases
While most locals also speak Dutch, English, or Spanish, learning a few Papiamentu phrases can go a long way in showing your appreciation for the culture. Here are some easy ones to get you started:
- Bon bini – Welcome
- Con ta bai? – How are you?
- Danki – Thank you
- Di nada – You're welcome

- Mi stima Boneiru – I love Bonaire

Locals are always delighted when visitors try to speak Papiamentu, even if it's just a word or two. Don't be shy—give it a try!

How It Shapes Bonairean Identity
Papiamentu is more than just a way to communicate; it's a living symbol of the island's history and resilience. It represents the blending of cultures that have influenced Bonaire over centuries, from the Indigenous Caquetío people to African, European, and Latin American settlers.

The language is also woven into local music, storytelling, and everyday expressions. Listen closely to the lyrics of traditional songs or the friendly banter at a local market, and you'll hear how Papiamentu adds color and rhythm to life on the island.

Why It Matters
In a world where smaller languages often fade away, Papiamentu remains strong. Schools teach it alongside Dutch, and efforts to preserve it are ongoing. By speaking it, locals keep their traditions alive, and visitors who embrace it get a richer, more authentic experience of Bonaire.

So the next time you step into a shop, greet someone with a cheerful "Bon dia" and see how quickly it sparks a smile. Papiamentu isn't just a language; it's an invitation to connect with the heart and soul of Bonaire.

Festivals, Music, and Art

Bonaire's culture comes alive through its vibrant festivals, music, and creative arts, offering visitors a chance to dive deeper into the island's traditions and community spirit. Life on the island is often celebrated through gatherings that showcase its unique blend of influences, from African roots to European and Caribbean heritage.

Festivals on Bonaire
Bonaire's calendar is dotted with festivals that highlight local culture, food, and music. If your visit coincides with one of these events, it's a great opportunity to experience the island at its liveliest.

Carnival
Carnival is one of the biggest celebrations on Bonaire, taking place in the weeks leading up to Lent. The island bursts into life with colorful parades, elaborate costumes, and infectious music. Events include the Grand Parade through Kralendijk, children's parades, and plenty of late-night parties. It's a time when the whole community comes together, and visitors are warmly welcomed to join the fun.

Dia di Rincon (Rincon Day)

Held every April 30 in Bonaire's oldest town, Rincon Day is a celebration of local traditions. The streets of Rincon fill with live music, dancing, and stalls selling traditional food and crafts. It's a fantastic way to experience the island's history and heritage.

Simadan (Harvest Festival)
This traditional festival honors Bonaire's agricultural roots. Taking place in spring, Simadan features songs, dances, and rituals that reflect the island's farming history. You might see locals dressed in traditional clothing performing dances that tell the story of planting and harvesting.

Regatta Week
Every October, Bonaire hosts an international sailing regatta that brings together sailors from across the Caribbean. While the races are the main event, the festival includes beach parties, live music, and a lively atmosphere in Kralendijk.

Music: The Sound of Bonaire
Music is the heartbeat of Bonaire's culture, blending African, Caribbean, and European influences. Traditional genres like Simadan music and Kriaoyo songs tell stories of the island's history and are often performed with instruments like drums, guitars, and the maraca-like kachu.

For a modern twist, you'll also hear plenty of reggae, salsa, and bachata at bars and beach clubs. Live music is a staple of the island's nightlife, so don't miss the chance to catch a local band or singer.

Art and Creativity
Bonaire's artistic scene is as colorful as its landscapes. Local artists draw inspiration from the island's natural beauty and cultural heritage, creating works that range from paintings and sculptures to handmade crafts.

Bonaire Arts & Crafts Market
Held weekly in Kralendijk, this market is a great place to meet local artists and pick up unique souvenirs. Look for paintings of Bonaire's landscapes, handmade jewelry, and wood carvings.

Mangazina di Rei
This cultural center near Rincon showcases Bonaire's history and traditions through exhibits and events. It's also a hub for local artisans, offering workshops on crafts like weaving and pottery.

Street Art in Kralendijk
Keep an eye out for murals and colorful street art as you walk through Kralendijk. These vibrant pieces often depict local life, marine themes, and the island's cultural pride.

Tips for Enjoying Bonaire's Culture

Ask Locals: They're often the best source for finding out about upcoming events or hidden artistic gems.

Bring Cash: Many markets and festivals are cash-only, so have some handy for buying crafts or snacks.

Join In: Don't be shy about dancing at a festival or asking about the meaning behind a song or artwork. Bonaireans are proud of their culture and happy to share it with visitors.

Bonaire's festivals, music, and art offer a window into the island's soul. Whether you're swaying to traditional rhythms, browsing local crafts, or celebrating alongside locals at a lively festival, you'll feel the warmth and creativity that make Bonaire so special.

The Influence of Dutch and Caribbean Heritage

Bonaire's culture is a fascinating blend of Dutch and Caribbean influences, reflecting its unique history and geography. This fusion is evident in the island's architecture, cuisine, language, and traditions, creating an identity that feels both rooted and cosmopolitan.

A Legacy of Dutch Colonialism

Bonaire has been part of the Kingdom of the Netherlands since the early 1600s, and you can still see Dutch influences throughout the island.

Architecture:
Walk through Kralendijk, and you'll spot brightly painted buildings with Dutch-style gabled roofs, a signature of colonial-era architecture. The pastel colors and simple designs are perfect for the tropical environment, blending practicality with charm.

Governance and Education:
As a special municipality of the Netherlands, Bonaire follows Dutch laws and systems. Dutch is one of the official languages, and schools on the island often teach in Dutch alongside Papiamentu.

Cuisine:
While local flavors dominate, you'll find hints of Dutch influence in Bonaire's food. Popular snacks like bitterballen (fried meatballs) and stroopwafels (thin waffle cookies with syrup) are a nod to the island's European ties.

Caribbean Roots and Vibrancy

Bonaire's Caribbean identity is equally strong, shaped by its Indigenous, African, and neighboring island influences.

Music and Dance:
Caribbean rhythms like reggae, calypso, and salsa dominate the island's music scene, but Bonaire adds its unique touch with traditional Simadan songs and dances that tell stories of the harvest.

Food and Flavors:
The island's cuisine showcases a Caribbean flair, with dishes like goat stew (kabritu), conch, and freshly caught fish served with plantains and funchi (a cornmeal side dish similar to polenta). Tropical fruits like mangoes and papayas are common in desserts and drinks.

Warmth and Hospitality:
Caribbean culture is all about community, and you'll feel it in the warm, welcoming attitude of Bonaireans. Locals are quick to share a story, offer a smile, or teach you a phrase in Papiamentu.

A Blend That Defines Bonaire

What makes Bonaire truly special is how seamlessly these Dutch and Caribbean elements come together. The island is a place where you can sip Dutch coffee in a Caribbean café, listen to reggae with a Papiamentu twist, and admire the combination of European design and island-inspired colors in the buildings.

Bonaire's dual heritage isn't just history—it's a living part of everyday life. By embracing both sides of its cultural identity, the island has created something uniquely its own. Visitors can experience this richness in every corner, whether they're exploring the capital, dining on local specialties, or chatting with a friendly local.

It's this harmonious blend that makes Bonaire more than just a destination—it's an experience where two worlds meet, creating something extraordinary.

9. Bonaire's Culinary Scene

Must-try dishes and local specialties

When it comes to food, Bonaire doesn't disappoint. The island's culinary scene is a flavorful reflection of its cultural heritage, blending Caribbean spices, Dutch influences, and fresh, local ingredients. Whether you're dining at a beachside eatery or a cozy family-owned spot, there's something for everyone to savor.

Local Favorites You Have to Try

Kabritu Stoba (Goat Stew)
This hearty dish is a must on Bonaire. Made with tender, slow-cooked goat meat in a rich, flavorful gravy, kabritu stoba is served with rice, plantains, or funchi (a polenta-like cornmeal side). It's a true taste of island tradition.

Fresh Seafood
Bonaire's waters are brimming with fresh fish like mahi-mahi, snapper, and tuna. Grilled, fried, or prepared in a tangy Creole sauce, seafood is a staple on most menus. Be sure to try lionfish—it's not only delicious but helps control the invasive species.

Sopi di Piska (Fish Soup)
This comforting soup is made with freshly caught fish, vegetables, and local herbs. It's a simple yet satisfying dish that showcases the island's reliance on the sea.

Funchi and Plantains
These classic sides are served with many meals. Funchi is a cornmeal-based dish, similar to polenta, and plantains are typically fried to a golden, caramelized perfection.

Pastechi
These flaky pastries are filled with cheese, meat, chicken, or fish and are a popular snack or breakfast item. You'll find them at local bakeries or roadside stands.

Sweet Treats and Desserts

Pan di Coco (Coconut Bread)
This soft, slightly sweet bread made with coconut is a delightful treat, perfect with a cup of tea or coffee.

Ponos di Kachó (Dog's Paws)
Despite the name, these are sugary, fried dough treats shaped like a paw. They're a favorite at festivals and markets.

Local Sorbet
Many restaurants and shops offer homemade sorbets made from tropical fruits like mango, tamarind, or passion fruit. Cool and refreshing, it's the perfect way to end a meal.

Drinks to Sip On

Cadushy Liqueur
Made from the cactus plant, this uniquely Bonairean liqueur has a smooth, slightly herbal flavor. Visit the Cadushy Distillery in Rincon for a tasting.

Rum Cocktails
Bonaireans know how to mix a great cocktail. Many bars serve tropical concoctions featuring local rums, perfect for sipping while watching the sunset.

Fresh Juices

Try fresh juice made from island fruits like tamarind, papaya, or passion fruit. It's a non-alcoholic treat that's full of natural flavor.

Where to Find These Dishes

Posada Para Mira in Rincon serves traditional dishes like kabritu stoba in a rustic, open-air setting.

It Rains Fishes in Kralendijk is known for its fresh seafood and laid-back atmosphere.

The Cadushy Distillery not only offers tastings but often sells small snacks and other local products.

Bonaire's culinary scene is a feast for the senses, with every dish telling a story of the island's culture and traditions. Whether you're indulging in a plate of fresh fish, savoring a sweet treat, or sipping on a tropical cocktail, you'll get a true taste of Bonaire's vibrant flavor.

Bonaire's culinary culture goes hand in hand with its connection to nature. The island's fresh seafood and growing farm-to-table movement make dining here a true celebration of local flavors.

Fresh Seafood: From Ocean to Plate

Bonaire's surrounding waters provide an abundance of fresh fish and shellfish that dominate many menus. Chefs on the island pride themselves on highlighting these ingredients with simple yet flavorful preparations.

Lionfish Delicacies
Lionfish may be an invasive species, but local efforts have turned this environmental challenge into a culinary opportunity. Many restaurants now serve lionfish in creative ways—grilled, fried, or even in ceviche. It's a mild, white fish that's both tasty and eco-friendly to eat.

Catch of the Day
Many eateries feature a "catch of the day," offering freshly caught mahi-mahi, wahoo, tuna, or snapper. It's often grilled and paired with island-inspired sauces like mango salsa or Creole sauce.

Shrimp and Lobster
While less common, shrimp and lobster dishes are a luxury you'll find at higher-end restaurants. These are often prepared with tropical spices or rich butter-based sauces.

Farm-to-Table Dining

While Bonaire's arid climate makes large-scale farming challenging, local growers and producers are finding innovative ways to bring fresh, sustainable ingredients to the table.

Bon Tera Farm
This local farm supplies many restaurants with fresh vegetables, herbs, and fruits. Bon Tera also hosts farm-to-table dinners where visitors can enjoy meals prepared with ingredients harvested just feet away from their plate.

Echotierra
This eco-friendly initiative focuses on organic farming and sustainable practices. They often collaborate with chefs for special events and dinners that highlight local produce.

Goat Farms
Goat farming is a tradition on Bonaire, and many farms now supply fresh goat cheese and milk to the island's culinary scene. Some even offer tours where you can see how these products are made.

Top Spots for Fresh and Local Dining

Brass Boer

Located at Delfins Beach Resort, this high-end restaurant by Dutch chefs Jonnie and Thérèse Boer offers a menu inspired by Bonaire's local produce and seafood. Their farm-to-table philosophy is evident in every dish.

Ocean Oasis

This beachfront restaurant offers a mix of fresh seafood and creative farm-to-table dishes. Their location is perfect for a sunset dinner.

Sebastian's

Known for its waterfront views and gourmet menu, Sebastian's sources local ingredients for dishes like lionfish and tropical fruit desserts.

Dining in Bonaire is more than just eating; it's about connecting with the island's land and sea. Every bite tells a story of sustainability, creativity, and tradition, whether you're enjoying a plate of grilled fish by the beach or attending a farm-to-table dinner under the stars.

10. Eco-Tourism and Sustainability

Bonaire's commitment to conservation

Bonaire isn't just a tropical getaway—it's a shining example of how tourism and sustainability can go hand in hand. The island has made preserving its natural beauty a top priority, and this dedication to conservation is part of what makes Bonaire so special.

A Leader in Marine Conservation
Bonaire has long been at the forefront of marine conservation. The Bonaire National Marine Park, established in 1979, protects the island's coral reefs, seagrass beds, and mangroves. This ensures that the waters surrounding Bonaire remain some of the healthiest and most vibrant in the world.

No Anchoring Policy: Boats are prohibited from anchoring on coral reefs. Instead, mooring buoys are provided to protect the fragile underwater ecosystems.

Marine Park Fee: Visitors pay a Nature Fee ($40 for divers and $20 for other users) that funds the maintenance and preservation of the park.

Spearheading Lionfish Control: Bonaire has taken an active role in managing the invasive lionfish population, encouraging local fishermen and divers to catch and consume the species.

Renewable Energy and Waste Management
Bonaire is also making strides on land to reduce its ecological footprint.

Wind Energy: Around 40% of Bonaire's electricity comes from wind turbines, significantly reducing the island's reliance on fossil fuels.

Plastic Reduction: Single-use plastics are being phased out, and many businesses encourage reusable bags, bottles, and straws.

Recycling Initiatives: Efforts to manage waste are ongoing, with local organizations promoting recycling and proper disposal methods.

Eco-Tourism Experiences
Bonaire's focus on sustainability extends to its tourism industry. Many activities and accommodations are designed to minimize environmental impact while giving visitors an authentic connection to nature.

Eco-Friendly Accommodations: Look for lodgings like Sorobon Beach Resort or Bamboo Bonaire, which use sustainable practices like solar power and water-saving technologies.
Mangrove Kayaking: Explore Bonaire's mangroves with eco-tours offered by Mangrove Center Bonaire. You'll learn about these vital ecosystems while paddling through calm, clear waters.

Wildlife Sanctuaries: Visit the Flamingo Sanctuary or the donkey sanctuary to support conservation efforts for Bonaire's unique animals.

Bonaire's commitment to conservation isn't just a trend—it's a way of life. The island's leaders and residents understand that protecting their natural resources is key to ensuring Bonaire remains a paradise for generations to come. As you explore its stunning landscapes and crystal-clear waters, you'll feel good knowing your visit supports these efforts.

How to Travel Sustainably on the Island

Bonaire's commitment to the environment is inspiring, and as a visitor, you can play a part in keeping this paradise pristine. Traveling sustainably doesn't require drastic changes—it's about making mindful choices that respect the island's ecosystems and culture.

Choose Eco-Friendly Accommodation

Many of Bonaire's hotels and guesthouses prioritize sustainability. Look for properties that use solar energy, conserve water, and minimize waste. Some even go the extra mile by offering reusable toiletries, on-site recycling, or discounts for guests who choose not to have daily housekeeping.

For example, **Bamboo Bonaire** uses solar panels and natural ventilation to reduce its carbon footprint. **Sorobon Beach** Resort incorporates sustainable practices while offering a cozy stay on the beach.

Minimize Plastic Use

Bonaire is working hard to reduce single-use plastics, so it's a great opportunity for you to join in.

- Bring your own reusable water bottle and fill it up with tap water, which is safe to drink.
- Carry a reusable shopping bag for souvenirs or groceries.
- Skip plastic straws and opt for biodegradable or reusable options, which many local businesses already provide.

Support Local Businesses

Traveling sustainably also means contributing to Bonaire's community. Spend your money at locally-owned shops, markets, and restaurants.

Choose tours run by locals who are passionate about the environment, like the Mangrove Center Bonaire, which offers eco-friendly kayaking trips.

Shop for handmade crafts and avoid souvenirs made from endangered species or coral.

Stick to Marked Trails

When exploring Bonaire's natural beauty, it's important to stay on designated paths and trails.

In Washington Slagbaai National Park, follow the marked routes to avoid damaging native plants or disturbing wildlife.

When hiking or caving, always go with a guide who knows the area and its preservation rules.

Drive Smart

If you're renting a car or scooter, consider combining activities to reduce your trips. While driving, stick to the main roads to avoid damaging fragile environments.

Many areas, like Kralendijk or Lac Bay, are bike-friendly, so you can leave the car behind altogether.

Be Mindful in the Water

Bonaire's marine life is spectacular, and protecting it is essential for the island's future.

- Always use reef-safe sunscreen to prevent harmful chemicals from damaging the coral.
- Avoid touching or standing on coral reefs—they're living organisms and can easily be harmed.
- If you're diving, keep your buoyancy under control to ensure you don't accidentally hit the reef.

Leave No Trace

This one's simple but powerful: whatever you bring, take it back with you. That includes trash, snacks, and anything else you carry around the island. If you see litter while you're out and about, consider picking it up—every small effort makes a difference.

Traveling sustainably on Bonaire isn't just about helping the environment—it's about connecting with the island in a more meaningful way. By making thoughtful choices, you're not only protecting its natural beauty but also showing respect for the people and traditions that make Bonaire such a unique destination. Your small actions can have a big impact, ensuring this slice of paradise stays just as magical for future visitors.

11. Practical Information for Travelers

Health and Safety Tips

Staying healthy and safe during your trip to Bonaire ensures you'll have nothing but wonderful memories to take home. While the island is incredibly welcoming and laid-back, a little preparation goes a long way.

Health Tips
Tap Water: Bonaire's tap water is safe to drink. It's desalinated seawater and has a clean, refreshing taste. Skip the bottled water and refill your reusable bottle instead.

Sun Protection: The Caribbean sun can be intense. Apply reef-safe sunscreen generously and wear a wide-brimmed hat and sunglasses when you're out and about. Lightweight, long-sleeved clothing can also protect you without overheating.

Hydration: Staying hydrated is essential, especially if you're diving, hiking, or spending hours in the sun. Drink water throughout the day, even if you don't feel thirsty.

Medical Services: Bonaire has a reliable medical center, Fundashon Mariadal, located in Kralendijk. It offers basic services and emergency care. For serious issues, evacuation to Curaçao or the Netherlands may be necessary, so consider travel insurance that covers this.

Mosquitoes: Although Bonaire is not known for malaria or other mosquito-borne illnesses, you'll still want to bring insect repellent, especially in the evenings or near mangroves.

Safety Tips

Low Crime Rate: Bonaire is generally very safe, but like anywhere, use common sense. Don't leave valuables in plain sight, especially in your car or on the beach.

Driving: Roads are generally well-maintained, but some areas, especially in Washington Slagbaai National Park, are unpaved and rugged. Drive cautiously and always carry a spare tire. If you're biking, watch out for uneven surfaces.

Diving Safety: Bonaire is a diver's paradise, but it's important to follow safety guidelines. Dive with a buddy, know your limits, and give yourself at least 24 hours before flying to avoid decompression sickness.

Wildlife Awareness: While the island's wildlife is mostly harmless, give animals their space. Donkeys and goats may wander onto roads, so stay alert when driving.

Swimming and Snorkeling: Be mindful of currents, especially at non-designated swimming areas. Always snorkel or swim with a buddy, and let someone know your plans.

Emergency Contacts
Police: Call 911 or 717-8000 for non-emergencies.
Ambulance: Dial 912 for immediate medical assistance.
Fire Department: Call 919 in case of a fire.
Tourist Hotline: For general assistance, you can reach the Tourism Corporation Bonaire at +599-717-8322.

Bonaire is a safe, relaxing destination, but these simple precautions ensure your trip goes smoothly. Take care of yourself, respect the island's natural beauty, and you'll leave with stories worth sharing.

Currency, Banking, and Costs

Understanding Bonaire's currency and costs will help you budget your trip and avoid any surprises. Here's a practical guide to handling money while you explore the island.

Currency in Bonaire

Bonaire uses the US Dollar (USD) as its official currency. This makes it incredibly convenient for travelers from the United States. Coins, including pennies, nickels, dimes, and quarters, are widely accepted, so be sure to hold on to your spare change—it'll come in handy for small purchases.

Banking and ATMs
- Banking Services: Major banks like MCB Bonaire (Maduro & Curiel's Bank) and Banco di Caribe offer full banking services.
- ATMs: You'll find ATMs across the island, especially in Kralendijk. These machines typically dispense US dollars and accept major credit and debit cards such as Visa and Mastercard. Look for ATMs near supermarkets, banks, and the airport.
- Fees: Some ATMs charge a fee for withdrawals, so check with your bank about international fees to avoid surprises.

Credit Cards and Cash
- Credit Cards: Credit and debit cards are widely accepted, especially at hotels, restaurants, and larger shops. However, smaller establishments, including local markets and food trucks, often prefer cash.
- Cash: Carrying some cash is a good idea, particularly for tips, small souvenirs, or purchases in rural areas.

Currency Exchange

If you're coming from a country that doesn't use US dollars, it's best to exchange your money before arriving or at the airport in Bonaire. Currency exchange services on the island are limited, and the rates may not always be favorable.

Costs in Bonaire

Bonaire is known for its laid-back vibe, but it's not necessarily a budget destination. Here's what you can expect to spend:

Meals: Dining out can range from $10–$15 for a casual meal to $50 or more for a fine dining experience. Local eateries, called "snacks," are great for affordable and tasty meals.

Accommodations: Budget lodgings start at around $80 per night, while mid-range hotels and resorts average $150–$300 per night. Luxury stays can exceed $400 per night.

Transportation: Car rentals cost $50–$75 per day. Bikes and scooters are less expensive options, averaging $10–$20 per day.

Activities: Diving is one of the pricier activities, with single tank dives costing around $50–$75. Guided tours and water sports vary in price, so it's worth comparing options.

Tips for Budgeting

Save on Food: Visit supermarkets like Van den Tweel or Warehouse Bonaire for affordable groceries. Cooking meals in your accommodation can help cut down on costs.

Plan Activities: Some natural attractions, like the beaches and flamingo sanctuary, are free to visit. For others, like Washington Slagbaai National Park, there's an entry fee ($45 for vehicles).

Nature Fee: Don't forget the mandatory Nature Fee ($40 for divers, $20 for other visitors), which supports conservation efforts.

By knowing what to expect, you can plan ahead and enjoy Bonaire without stressing about finances. A mix of cash and card, along with mindful budgeting, ensures a smooth and enjoyable experience on this stunning island.

Local Customs and Etiquette

Bonaire's warm and friendly atmosphere comes with a strong sense of community and cultural pride. Understanding local customs and etiquette can help you connect with the island's people and show respect for their traditions.

Greetings and Politeness

A Warm "Bon dia": In Bonaire, a friendly greeting goes a long way. Use phrases like "Bon dia" (Good morning), "Bon tardi" (Good afternoon), or "Bon nochi" (Good evening) when meeting someone.

Eye Contact and Handshakes: A smile, direct eye contact, and a light handshake are standard ways to greet people. For those you know well, a kiss on the cheek is common.

Punctuality

Life on Bonaire runs at a relaxed pace, and people tend to be more flexible about time. However, if you have an appointment, tour, or dinner reservation, it's still polite to arrive on time.

Respect for the Environment

Locals take great pride in their island's natural beauty. Avoid littering and follow eco-friendly practices, such as using reef-safe sunscreen and sticking to marked trails in natural areas.

Be mindful of coral: Don't touch or step on the coral when snorkeling or diving—it's fragile and takes decades to recover from damage.

Dining Etiquette

Tipping: Tipping isn't mandatory but is appreciated. A service charge may be included in your bill (typically 10–15%), so check before adding a tip. If no service charge is listed, 10–20% is a good guideline for restaurants. For taxi drivers and guides, rounding up the fare or adding a small amount is customary.

Casual Atmosphere: Dining in Bonaire is generally laid-back. There's no need to dress formally unless you're visiting an upscale restaurant.

Wait for the Check: In many restaurants, you'll need to ask for the check when you're ready to leave—it won't be brought automatically.

Modesty and Dress

While beachwear is fine for the shore, it's respectful to cover up when walking through town or dining at restaurants. Lightweight clothing like sundresses, shorts, and T-shirts are perfect for the island's climate.

Driving Etiquette

Drive cautiously and follow local speed limits (usually 30–60 km/h).

Use your horn sparingly; it's considered impolite unless used to alert someone for safety reasons.

Be patient with the island's free-roaming donkeys and goats—they often wander onto the roads.

Photography

Ask permission before photographing locals, especially in smaller communities. Most people are friendly and willing, but it's a good practice to show respect by asking first.

Respecting Cultural Events

If you're lucky enough to visit during a festival or celebration, such as Carnival, enjoy the music and dancing but remember to be respectful of traditions. Participate with enthusiasm, but always follow the lead of locals.

By embracing Bonaire's customs and showing courtesy, you'll not only enhance your experience but also leave a positive impression on the community. The people of Bonaire are known for their kindness and hospitality, and a little effort to understand their way of life goes a long way.

12. Suggested Itineraries

A Three-Day Highlights Tour

If you've only got three days to explore Bonaire, don't worry—you can still experience its charm, natural beauty, and vibrant culture. This itinerary balances adventure, relaxation, and some local flavor to give you the best of the island.

Day 1: Dive into the Island's Best

Morning:
Start with breakfast in Kralendijk: Head to Between 2 Buns for fresh pastries, smoothies, and delicious sandwiches. Their coffee will kick-start your day.
Explore Bonaire National Marine Park: Rent snorkel or dive gear from Dive Friends Bonaire (divefriendsbonaire.com) or Buddy Dive Resort (buddydive.com). Spend the morning exploring world-renowned underwater sites like 1000 Steps or Salt Pier. You'll be mesmerized by the colorful corals and marine life.

Afternoon:

Lunch with a view: Enjoy a laid-back meal at Ocean Oasis Beach Club, where fresh seafood and tropical cocktails come with oceanfront seating.
Flamingos and salt flats: Visit Pekelmeer Flamingo Sanctuary to see these graceful birds in their natural habitat. Nearby, the pink salt flats offer unique photo opportunities.

Evening:
Dine in style: Book a table at It Rains Fishes for fresh, locally-sourced seafood dishes paired with an elegant yet relaxed atmosphere.

Day 2: Outdoor Adventures

Morning:
Kayak through mangroves: Join a guided tour with Mangrove Center Bonaire (mangrovecenter.com) to paddle through the lush mangroves of Lac Bay. It's an unforgettable way to connect with nature.
Relax at Lac Bay: Stay in the area and watch windsurfers glide across the turquoise waters. Beginners can take a lesson at Jibe City (jibecity.com) or just lounge at the beach.

Afternoon:
Lunch at Sorobon Beach Resort: Feast on local flavors while soaking in the serene views of Lac Bay.
Discover caves: Explore Bonaire's limestone caves with Flow Bonaire Tours (flowbonaire.com). These fascinating formations are a hidden treasure on the island.

Evening:
Sunset vibes: Catch the sunset at Te Amo Beach. Bring a blanket, some snacks, and a drink—it's a perfect spot to wind down.

Day 3: Culture and History

Morning:
Breakfast with a local twist: Try local Johnny cakes and coffee at Karel's Beach Bar.
Stroll through Kralendijk: Visit the colorful market stalls and shops along Kaya Grandi. Don't miss the Bonaire Museum of History, which provides a fascinating glimpse into the island's past.

Afternoon:

Lunch at Posada Para Mira: This family-run restaurant in Rincon serves hearty, authentic Bonairean dishes like goat stew and plantains.

Explore Rincon: Visit the historic village of Rincon, Bonaire's oldest settlement. Stop by Cadushy Distillery to taste the island's unique cactus liqueur and learn about its production.

Evening:

Farewell dinner: For your last evening, treat yourself to a memorable dining experience at Brass Boer, located at Delfins Beach Resort (delfinsbeachresort.com). The menu blends local ingredients with innovative techniques, offering a true culinary adventure.

This three-day plan gives you a taste of Bonaire's stunning landscapes, adventurous activities, and rich culture. With plenty of room for relaxation, it's the perfect way to make the most of a short visit to this Caribbean gem.

Tailored Plans for Divers, Families, and Nature Enthusiasts

If you're looking for a more personalized experience, Bonaire offers something special for every type of traveler. Here's how you can tailor your itinerary based on your interests.

For Divers: Immersing in the Marine Wonderland

Day 1: Shore Diving Extravaganza
Morning: Head straight to Buddy Dive Resort (buddydive.com) to rent your gear. Start your underwater adventure with a dive at The Hilma Hooker, a famous shipwreck teeming with marine life.
Afternoon: Grab lunch at Kite City Food Truck, conveniently located near Donkey Beach, and then enjoy an afternoon dive at Bari Reef, one of the most biodiverse spots in the Caribbean.
Evening: Reflect on your day with a group of fellow divers over dinner at Dive Inn Bonaire.

Day 2: Boat Diving and Exploration
Book a day of boat diving with Caribbean Dive Academy (caribbeandiveacademy.com). They'll take you to Klein Bonaire, a pristine uninhabited islet with incredible dive sites like No Name Beach and Hands Off Reef.
After your dives, enjoy a relaxed dinner at Cuba Compagnie, known for its lively atmosphere and fusion dishes.

Day 3: Diving Freedom
End your trip with self-guided shore dives at iconic sites like 1000 Steps or Salt Pier. Dive at your own pace and soak up every last moment.

For Families: Relaxation and Fun

Day 1: Family-Friendly Exploration
Morning: Kick off your vacation with a trip to Donkey Sanctuary Bonaire. Kids will love feeding and interacting with the friendly donkeys.
Afternoon: Have a picnic lunch at Bachelor's Beach, where the shallow waters are perfect for young swimmers.
Evening: Enjoy a casual dinner at Pasa Bon Pizza, offering kid-friendly options and a relaxed atmosphere.

Day 2: Active Adventures
Morning: Book a family kayaking tour with Bonaire Eco Adventure (bonaireecoadventure.com) to explore the mangroves.
Afternoon: Head to Jibe City at Lac Bay, where kids can try windsurfing or just play in the shallow water while parents relax on the beach.
Evening: Enjoy a sunset dinner at Sebastian's, known for its stunning ocean views and varied menu.

Day 3: Cultural Discovery
Spend the morning exploring the markets and shops in Kralendijk. Let the kids pick out souvenirs and local crafts.
Visit Terramar Museum to learn about the island's history, followed by lunch at Boudoir Bonaire, which has a cozy and family-friendly vibe.

For Nature Enthusiasts: Exploring Bonaire's Wild Side

Day 1: National Park Adventures
Spend the entire day exploring Washington Slagbaai National Park. Hike to natural landmarks like Brandaris, snorkel at remote beaches, and keep an eye out for flamingos. Pack plenty of water and snacks, as the park is expansive.

In the evening, unwind with a hearty meal at Karel's Beach Bar, which offers fresh seafood and outdoor seating.

Day 2: Mangroves and Wildlife
Start with a guided kayak tour through Lac Bay's mangroves with Mangrove Center Bonaire (mangrovecenter.com). Learn about this vital ecosystem and its role in the island's biodiversity.
Spend the afternoon birdwatching at Gotomeer Lagoon, where you'll see flamingos, herons, and other species.
Wrap up the day with dinner at La Cantina Cerveceria, known for its garden setting and locally brewed craft beer.

Day 3: Caving and Stargazing
Explore Bonaire's unique limestone caves with Flow Bonaire Tours (flowbonaire.com). Marvel at the ancient formations and learn about their geological history.
In the evening, join a stargazing tour with a local guide. Bonaire's minimal light pollution makes it a fantastic destination for astronomy enthusiasts.

Whether you're diving deep into Bonaire's marine park, enjoying family fun at the beach, or immersing yourself in nature, these tailored plans ensure you experience the island in a way that suits your style.

Accommodations

Bonaire offers a variety of accommodations to suit different budgets and preferences, ranging from luxurious beachfront resorts to cozy apartments and eco-friendly lodges. Below is a selection of options with approximate rates and contact details to help you find the perfect place to stay.

Luxury Stays

Harbour Village Beach Club

Highlights: Private beach, on-site diving center, and upscale amenities. Ideal for those seeking exclusivity and tranquility.
Rates: Starting at $425 per night for a standard room.
Contact: Visit harbourvillage.com or call +599-717-7500.

Delfins Beach Resort
Highlights: Modern design, beachfront setting, and a world-class restaurant (Brass Boer). Perfect for couples and foodies.
Rates: Starting at $320 per night.
Contact: Visit delfinsbeachresort.com or call +599-717-7070.

Mid-Range Options

Buddy Dive Resort

Highlights: Dive-focused resort with excellent facilities, including gear rentals and guided dives.
Rates: Rooms start at $180 per night.
Contact: Visit buddydive.com or call +599-717-5080.

The Bellafonte Luxury Oceanfront Hotel
Highlights: Oceanfront property offering spacious suites and personalized service.
Rates: Starting at $250 per night.
Contact: Visit bellafontebonaire.com or call +599-717-3333.

Budget-Friendly Options

Bamboo Bonaire Boutique Resort

Highlights: Charming boutique resort with lush gardens, a pool, and friendly hosts.
Rates: Starting at $120 per night.

Contact: Visit bamboobonaire.com or call +599-786-3637.

Bonaire Backpackers
Highlights: Affordable and simple, great for solo travelers or those on a tight budget.
Rates: Starting at $25 per night for a dorm bed.
Contact: Visit bonairebackpackers.com or call +599-701-0637.

Eco-Friendly Stays

Eco Lodge Bonaire
Highlights: Sustainable lodging with solar energy and eco-conscious practices. Located in a serene setting near nature trails.
Rates: Starting at $100 per night.
Contact: Visit ecolodgebonaire.com or call +599-788-2677.

Sorobon Beach Resort

Highlights: Perfect for nature lovers, with cozy beach cottages located steps from Lac Bay.
Rates: Starting at $200 per night.
Contact: Visit sorobonbeachresort.com or call +599-701-7777.

Vacation Rentals

Kas di Laman Apartments
Highlights: Self-catering apartments in a central location, ideal for longer stays.
Rates: Starting at $110 per night.
Contact: Visit kasdilaman.com or call +599-785-3115.

Bonaire Sunset Villa
Highlights: A private villa with breathtaking sunset views, perfect for families or groups.
Rates: Starting at $350 per night.
Contact: Visit bonairevillas.com or call +599-717-7362.

Tips for Choosing Accommodation
Proximity to Attractions: If you plan to dive frequently, consider staying near Kralendijk or a resort with easy access to dive sites.

Transportation: Many accommodations offer car rental packages, which can simplify exploring the island.

Early Booking: Bonaire is a popular destination, especially during peak diving seasons (December to April). Book early to secure your preferred stay.

From budget-friendly havens to luxurious beachfront escapes, Bonaire's accommodations cater to every traveler's needs. Be sure to check for special deals and packages that include activities like diving or windsurfing for added value.

We'd Love to Hear From You

Are you enjoying this travel guide? Your thoughts and feedback are incredibly valuable to us. We want to make sure this book truly enhances your journey and provides the insights you're looking for.

If you have a moment, we'd be so grateful if you could share your honest feedback. It's easy—just scan the QR code to leave your feedback. Your input not only helps us improve but also guides other travelers like you.

Thank you for being a part of this adventure and for helping us make future editions even better!

Made in United States
North Haven, CT
12 February 2025

65730343R00043